I feel calm

When I feel calm my body is still and my thoughts are peaceful. **It's like floating on a cloud.**

If my heart is beating fast and my body feels tense, I take three deep breaths, in through my nose and out through my mouth. As my breathing slows down, my arms and legs feel more loose; I am calm.

Sitting by a warm, cosy fire, or looking up at a starry sky always makes me feel calm.

My dog feels frisky!

When I come home from school, my dog gets excited. **He's so happy to see me** that he even looks as though he's smiling. Sometimes he gets so frisky, he'll pick up his favourite toy, shake it and then fling it high up in the air.

Feeling goofy, silly and full of energy is a happy feeling.

I feel cosy!

I feel so cosy when I snuggle up in bed with my favourite doll, Ruby. Being tucked under a soft, fluffy blanket makes me feel warm and comfy; especially when it's cold outside. **There's nothing better than cuddling up close to someone you love;** it makes you feel safe and all fuzzy inside. **Now that is cosy!**

What makes you feel cosy?

I'm a grumpy bear!

When **I'm in a bad mood**, my mum calls me a 'grumpy bear'. If I'm grumpy, I get grouchy and sometimes... **I even growl!** I sulk and say mean things to people. Everybody gets grumpy at some time but you have to do something about it. If I find a quiet corner to sit or go for a walk that helps me to get rid of the 'grumpy bear' feeling.

What do you do when you feel like this?

Mr. Sloth

I feel lazy. **I just want to lie around and do nothing at all.** Sometimes when you feel lazy, you have to just get up and get moving to get things done. It's okay to be quiet and lazy once in a while, but when it's time to get going, it's time to get going.

Do you ever feel lazy?

13

Anticipation!

Mike winds up the handle of his Jack-in-the-Box. As the music starts to play, he gets so excited waiting for Jack to jump out of the box. When he does, the look of surprise on Mike's face makes everybody laugh. When you're excited about something that is going to happen it's called anticipation. **It's the feeling you get the night before your birthday** when you can't wait to open your presents.

When did you last feel like this?

15

I'm so disappointed!

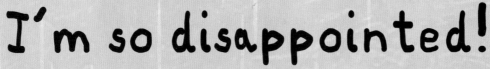

Have you ever really, really wanted to do something but then you couldn't do it? The feeling you get when this happens is called disappointment.

My best friend and I planned to go to the park today, but **we couldn't go because there was a big thunderstorm – we were so disappointed.**

But instead of being sad, we found something else to do that was good fun.

What do you do when you feel disappointed?

18

I'm so pleased!

My shiny red car is waiting for the race to start. The flag drops and... they're off! My car zooms along, **trying hard** to pass the others. After four exciting laps, it wins the race. I'm so pleased with my little car **because it worked so hard to win**... and it did!

What makes you feel pleased?

I feel safe

My mum and dad make me feel safe, **because they are always there for me.** They look after me if I'm ill; they let me sleep in their bed if I have a scary dream; and they always make sure my car seatbelt is buckled. They make me feel safe.

What makes you feel safe?

Guilty!

If you do something that you know you're not supposed to do – like telling a lie – it makes you feel bad. When my puppy gets caught stealing something or chewing my shoe, he knows it's wrong. He feels guilty. He looks at me with his big eyes, his ears go droopy and he tucks his tail between his legs. If you ever feel guilty about something you've done, try to make it right.

And then try not to do it again!

I feel joyful!

When the sun is shining and the birds are singing, it makes the day feel joyful, happy and free. Being joyful is a good feeling. **Every day it's good to find one thing that makes you feel happy and joyful.**

It makes you smile!

Jealousy is bad for you...

When someone else has something that you really want, it can make you feel jealous. I only got a 'B' for my homework and Katie got an 'A'. I was really jealous. Sometimes when I get jealous, I say mean things and that usually makes me feel worse. **It's not good to be mean to people.**

Try to be happy with what you have, instead.

I feel tense

If you stretch an elastic band as far as you can – it feels rigid. I feel like that when I go to the dentist because I feel a bit scared. I can't relax and **my muscles feel tight and stiff – just like the elastic band!**

If I take deep breaths it helps my muscles to relax.

Sometimes I feel worried

Sometimes I worry about lots of things, like my next maths test, or telling my brother that I've broken his bike.

Feeling worried or scared about something is not a good feeling. **You need to work out how to make things better.** So... if I work harder at my maths and tell my brother what I've done, my worries will go away.

What do you worry about?

It's so frustrating

My spinning top wants to keep going but it always slows down and stops. Sometimes, no matter how hard I try, I just can't do something. I get so cross and frustrated that I just want to give up. But maybe, if I keep on trying – I'll succeed!

What makes you feel like this?

Feeling loved...

Mother Duck takes good care of her baby ducklings. She paddles slowly down the river with them and **always makes sure they feel safe and happy.** Every day, Mother Duck tells her ducklings how much she loves them. It always feels good to know that somebody loves you.

Who makes you feel loved?

I felt ashamed...

It feels really horrible when you know that you've done something wrong. I blamed my friend for something she didn't do and she got into trouble for it. **I felt ashamed** of myself **because I was so sorry for what I did.**

Saying 'sorry' can sometimes make things better again.

The silly clown!

Clowns are always silly! They try to make us laugh, by tripping over their big feet, wearing colourful clothes and making funny faces. When I feel silly, **it feels like there's a bubble in my tummy.** When it suddenly bursts, I giggle and dance around all wild and crazy.

It's okay to be silly once in a while.

All alone...

I'm all alone. There's nobody around and it's too quiet. I don't like that feeling. Sometimes, you can even feel lonely when you're surrounded by a group of people! I go over to my friend's house or ask my brother or sister to play with me if I feel lonely.

What do you do if you feel lonely?

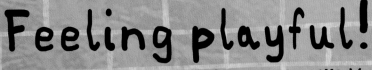

Feeling playful!

Have you ever seen kittens sit still? Me neither! My kittens are always running around, chasing their tails, pouncing on each other and wrestling. Sometimes kittens get so lively that they get into mischief, like getting tangled up in a ball of wool.

Feeling playful is good for you!

I'm fuming mad!

Have you ever seen a kettle boiling? Steam billows everywhere and the lid looks as though it's going to pop off! Being fuming mad is a problem though – because it's worse than just feeling mad. **It feels like you might explode.** Try taking some deep breaths to relax your body.

You can't solve a problem when you're full of anger.

Mischievous Ricky

Ricky the Raccoon loves to explore but **sometimes his curiosity gets him into trouble.** When he goes looking for yummy snacks in the rubbish bin, he sometimes knocks it over. He feels playful, sneaky and a little naughty all at the same time.

Do you ever feel mischievous?

I'm so thankful!

I bring my teddy bear with me to school. He makes me feel happy because I know I'm not alone. It's so good to see him snuggled in my backpack on the bus run to school. He makes me feel so happy that I can't stop saying 'Thank you'. **Feeling thankful gives me a warm feeling.**

It's important to show that you're thankful with a hug, a smile or even a note.

I was brave!

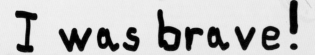

I **had to do something that was really hard**, but I knew that it was the right thing to do. I had to be brave. I had lost my sister's favourite bracelet and it took a lot of courage for me to tell her about it. My sister was sad about her bracelet, but she was pleased that I had told her the truth.

Some things are really hard to do, but you know you have to do them.

I feel heartbroken

I once felt so sad that it felt like my heart was breaking – it hurt! My dog Rusty got poorly and didn't get better. I was so upset and thought I would never smile again. My friends tried to make me feel better, but no matter what they did or said, nothing helped. **I couldn't stop crying.** As time passed I started to remember the times we spent together and it made me feel better.

I will never forget Rusty.

I feel intimidated

Every lunchtime, Billy the Bully comes to my table and gives me a mean, scary look. He wants the biscuits in my lunch box. I want them too, but Billy scares me with his mean voice. Feeling intimidated like this, or scared, is not a good feeling. I don't know what to do?

When you feel like this you need to ask an adult for help.

I'm bored!

There's nothing to do and nothing interesting going on – I'm bored! I suppose everybody gets bored once in a while. It's up to me to do something about it or my whole day will be boring! I'll try to think of something new to do – something I've never done before...

Once you find something to do, you soon forget that you were ever bored.

75

Feeling strong

The wind howls through the desert and moves everything in its path except for one tall tree. The tree bends in the wind but it has strong roots and doesn't move. The desert fox is glad of its shelter. This tree is strong.

Have you ever felt strong and powerful?

Contented as a sleeping baby

A sleeping baby always looks content. When my brother is sleeping, he looks so peaceful and happy. Just before he goes to bed he has a warm bath and then he's fed. He's warm and comfy in his cot and his tummy is full. My brother has everything he needs so he's content.

What makes you feel content?

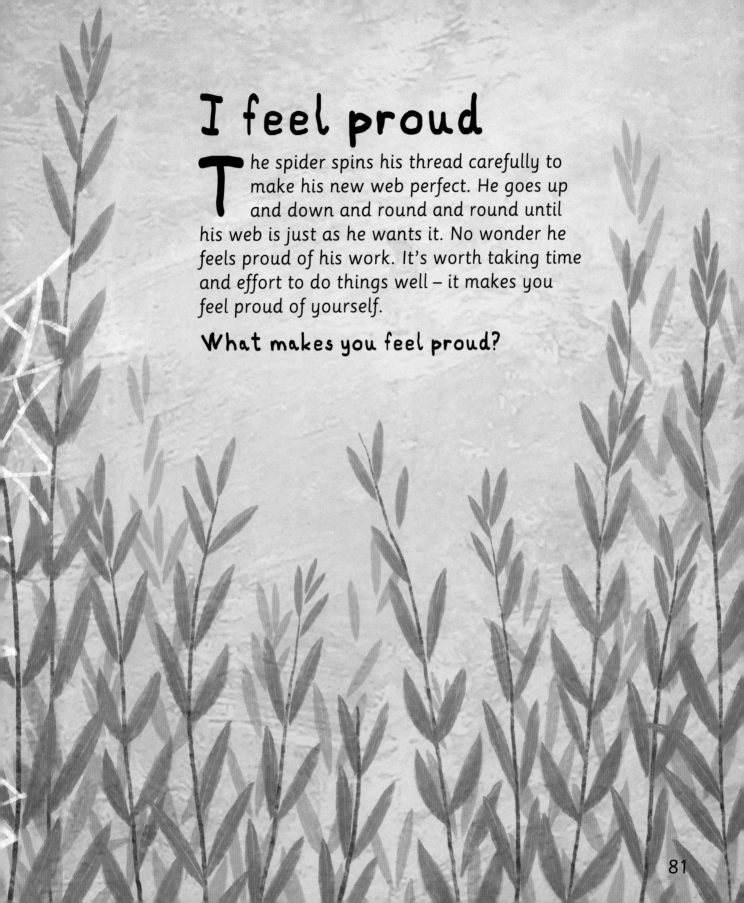

I feel proud

The spider spins his thread carefully to make his new web perfect. He goes up and down and round and round until his web is just as he wants it. No wonder he feels proud of his work. It's worth taking time and effort to do things well – it makes you feel proud of yourself.

What makes you feel proud?

Sometimes Harry wants to be alone

My pet turtle Harry goes into his shell when he wants to be alone and away from people. It's peaceful in his shell so he stays there until he feels like playing again.

At first I thought Harry didn't want to be my friend, but now I know that **he needs to be alone sometimes.**

When he's ready, he'll come out again.

I feel stupid!

Have you ever felt stupid trying to do something new? I have! When I was learning to tap dance, my shoes felt funny, it was hard to walk and I kept tripping over my own feet. But after a lot of practice, things got easier and I'm good at tap dancing now. Today I'm learning to ice-skate!

Have you ever felt stupid doing something new?

I feel rotten!

I've eaten too many sweets and now I feel yucky! I feel terrible because I ate too much, but also because I didn't listen to my mum. **Doing something you know you shouldn't have done just makes things worse.** Next time maybe I'll listen to my mum.

Have you ever wished that you hadn't done something?

I'm sorry!

Have you ever done something that you didn't mean to do? I've just tripped over my friend's block tower and broken it. **I feel sad because I've ruined his tower and hurt his feelings.** I said I was sorry and would be more careful next time.

We rebuilt the tower together — that helped to make everything right again.

Curiosity

Babies are curious about everything. My baby sister loves to crawl about and explore the world. She touches everything, smells things and sometimes puts the oddest things in her mouth. Being curious is good fun – it helps us to learn about new things.

Are you curious?

Feelings, feelings, feelings!

Everybody has feelings. There are good feelings like being happy, surprised, and excited, and problem ones like feeling sad, mad and frustrated. **When you have happy feelings enjoy them!** And when you have a bad feeling, you need to solve the problem yourself, or with help, so that you will feel better.

But no matter how you are feeling, that feeling belongs to you.

How do you feel today?

Published in Great Britain in MMXVIII by
Book House, an imprint of
The Salariya Book Company Ltd
25 Marlborough Place, Brighton BN1 1UB

www.salariya.com

ISBN: 978-1-912233-36-6

SCRIBO   BOOK HOUSE   SCRIBBLERS

1 3 5 7 9 8 6 4 2

Author: Jennifer Moore-Mallinos
Illustrations: Gustavo Mazali
Design and layout: Estudi Guasch, S.L
All rights reserved.
© Gemser Publications, S.L. 2017
El Castell, 38 08329 Teià (Barcelona, Spain)
www.mercedesros.com

English text © The Salariya Book Company Ltd MMXVIII

A CIP catalogue record for this book is available
from the British Library.

Printed and bound in China.

Visit
www.salariya.com
for our online catalogue and
free fun stuff.